MW00614098

FAIRIES

Martha London

DiscoverRoo
An Imprint of Pop!
popbooksonline.com

abdobooks.com

Published by Pop!, a division of ABDO, PO Box 398166, Minneapolis, Minnesota 55439. Copyright © 2020 by POP, LLC. International copyrights reserved in all countries. No part of this book may be reproduced in any form without written permission from the publisher. Pop!™ is a trademark and logo of POP, LLC.

Printed in the United States of America, North Mankato, Minnesota.

102019
012020

THIS BOOK CONTAINS RECYCLED MATERIALS

Cover Photo: Shutterstock Images
Interior Photos: Shutterstock Images, 1, 13, 14 (top), 15 (top), 15 (bottom), 17, 21 (pixie), 21 (brownie), 24, 25; iStockphoto, 5, 6, 9, 10, 11, 12, 18, 19, 21 (leprechaun), 21 (pot of gold), 21 (broom), 23, 28–29, 30, 31; yon marsh Phototrix/Alamy, 7; The Print Collector/Alamy, 14 (bottom); Pictures Now/Alamy, 26–27

Editor: Sophie Geister-Jones
Series Designer: Jake Nordby

Library of Congress Control Number: 2019942483

Publisher's Cataloging-in-Publication Data

Names: London, Martha, author.

Title: Fairies / by Martha London

Description: Minneapolis, Minnesota : Pop!, 2020 | Series: Mythical creatures | Includes online resources and index.

Identifiers: ISBN 9781532165757 (lib. bdg.) | ISBN 9781532167072 (ebook)

Subjects: LCSH: Mythical animals--Juvenile literature. | Fairies--Juvenile literature. | Folklore--Juvenile literature | Legends--Juvenile literature. | Animals and history--Juvenile literature.

Classification: DDC 398.45--dc23

WELCOME TO DiscoverRoo!

Pop open this book and you'll find QR codes loaded with information, so you can learn even more!

Scan this code* and others like it while you read, or visit the website below to make this book pop!

popbooksonline.com/fairies

*Scanning QR codes requires a web-enabled smart device with a QR code reader app and a camera.

TABLE OF
CONTENTS

CHAPTER 1
DANCING WITH FAIRIES

Three girls follow a path deep in the forest. The moon shines through the trees. Suddenly, the girls see flickering lights ahead. A group of fairies are dancing in a **clearing**. They leap and

WATCH A VIDEO HERE!

Many stories say fairies live in forests or other natural areas.

twirl in a circle. The fairies invite the girls

to join them.

The girls step into the circle. But it
is a trap. The girls are forced to dance
all night. Suddenly, the fairies vanish.

DID YOU KNOW? Circles of mushrooms are called fairy rings. Some legends say the rings are portals to the world of fairies.

The girls sit in a circle of mushrooms. It is morning. The girls are surprised. But they're lucky to be back. Sometimes fairies keep people forever.

Fairy rings can be found all over the world. This ring is in Ireland.

CHAPTER 2
ANCIENT FAIRIES

Legends about fairies have existed for thousands of years. Nearly every country has stories of fairy-like creatures. But most stories of fairies come from Western Europe. In England, stories about fairies date back to the 1100s.

LEARN MORE HERE!

Water sprites are fairies that
live in or near water.

Fairies play tricks on humans and on one another.

10

Many fairy stories had **morals**.
These lessons taught children how to
behave. Some stories said fairies could
cause bad things to happen. These
stories were meant to protect people.
They kept people away from dangerous
places, such as tall mountains and dark
forests.

Most fairies like living in the wild more than living in towns.

For many years, people believed in and feared fairies. But in the 1800s, ideas about fairies began to change. More stories described fairies as friendly to

DID YOU KNOW? In 1927, Britain formed the Fairy Investigation Society. This group tracked down stories of fairy sightings.

humans. These gentle fairies were often very small and beautiful.

In 1917, Elsie Wright and Frances Griffiths made cutouts of fairies from a book. The girls took turns taking pictures with the fairies. They showed the pictures to their families. It was supposed to be a joke. But Elsie's mother believed the photos were real. For many years, some people used the photos as **evidence** that fairies were real. In the 1980s, however, Elsie admitted that the photos were a **hoax**.

FAIRIES THROUGH THE YEARS

700

Early stories describe leprechauns as water spirits. They don't yet guard gold.

700s

Irish monks begin writing down Irish fairy stories.

1100

English folk tales of fairies are written. These fairies are wild and sometimes violent.

1974

The game Dungeons and Dragons is created. This game includes beautiful, delicate fairy characters.

1904

The fairy Tinker Bell first appears in the play *Peter Pan*.

1812

The Brothers Grimm publish a collection of stories including Cinderella and her fairy godmother.

15

CHAPTER 3
TYPES OF FAIRIES

In many stories, fairies look like small

humans. They often have pointed ears.

However, there are many kinds of fairies.

They include pixies, leprechauns, and

brownies. Each kind of fairy has its own

look and abilities.

The clothes a fairy wears often depend on where the fairy lives.

COMPLETE AN ACTIVITY HERE!

Pixies are some of the tiniest fairies.

They have beautiful wings. Some stories

say their wings look like a butterfly's.

Leprechauns are short and have beards. Leprechauns guard pots of gold. Legends say you can find them at the end of a rainbow.

Leprechauns appear in many Irish legends.

Brownies are small fairies that live in people's homes. Brownies usually have brown skin and are covered in hair. Unlike pixies, brownies and leprechauns do not have wings.

PIXIE

wings

pointed ears

DID YOU KNOW? Many types of fairies can make themselves disappear.

LEPRECHAUN

pot of gold

beard

BROWNIE

lots of hair

broom

CHAPTER 4
TRICKSTERS OR HELPERS

Each type of fairy has its own personality.

Some fairies are **mischievous**. They

like to play tricks on people. Sometimes

the tricks are **harmless**. For example,

pixies can trick travelers into going the

LEARN MORE HERE!

Tooth fairies trade lost teeth for money.

wrong direction. When the magic wears

off, the travelers have to turn around.

Other actions are more harmful. For example, some fairies use music to lead people to the fairy world. They may keep humans trapped for years.

Irish legends say that fairies taught humans how to play music.

In other stories, fairies kidnap

children. The fairy switches a human

child with a fairy child. The human lives

Fairies offered many gifts, including human children, to their kings and queens.

forever in the fairy world. The fairy child

is called a changeling. This child is left

with the stolen baby's family.

Not all fairies are bad. Brownies are helpful. During the night, they clean the homes of humans. They wash the dishes and tidy the rooms. But families must leave a chair by the fireplace. It gives brownies a place to rest.

DID YOU KNOW?

One level of Girl Scouts are called brownies. They are named after the helpful creatures.

Today, people may make fairy houses for their gardens or yards.

MAKING CONNECTIONS

TEXT-TO-SELF

If you saw a fairy circle, would you check it out or leave it alone?

TEXT-TO-TEXT

Have you ever read a fictional story about fairies? How did those fairies look and act?

TEXT-TO-WORLD

Many fairy stories were created to teach children lessons. What is one lesson that might help keep children safe?

GLOSSARY

clearing – an area that does not have trees.

evidence – facts that show whether a statement or story is true.

harmless – not dangerous.

hoax – a trick.

mischievous – enjoying the act of playing tricks on people.

moral – a lesson that teaches people about what is right or wrong.

INDEX

ONLINE RESOURCES
popbooksonline.com

Scan this code* and others like it while you read, or visit the website below to make this book pop!

popbooksonline.com/fairies

*Scanning QR codes requires a web-enabled smart device with a QR code reader app and a camera.